A Full Day!

By Sally Cowan

Dad, Tish and Tuck went camping.

Dad pulled back the flap of the tent.

Can I go for a swim?
Can I bring my ball?

"We can walk up
that tall hill!" said Dad.
"Then we can swim
and play with the ball."

Tuck had a fall
and rolled in some mud.

Then Tish hit a bug nest.
Small bugs buzzed out of it!

"I got a sting!" called Tish.

That was such a **bad** walk!
Let's all have a rest.

“Is it a bad sting?” said Dad.

“It’s a small sting,” said Tish.
“I am OK.”

Tuck played with his ball.

CHECKING FOR MEANING

1. Where do Dad, Tish and Tuck plan to walk to? *(Literal)*
2. Who falls and rolls in mud? *(Literal)*
3. Did the kids want to go for a walk? *(Inferential)*

EXTENDING VOCABULARY

flap	What is a flap on a tent? What would you call this in a house?
called	What other word could the author have used instead of *called*? If you call, are you using a soft or a loud voice?
full	Read the word *full*. What are the sounds in this word? Why was the family's day full?

MOVING BEYOND THE TEXT

1. Why do people like walking in nature? What might you see on a walk in your neighbourhood?
2. Would you like to go on a bush walk? Why?
3. How can you prepare for a big walk? What equipment or snacks might you need?
4. What are some other outdoor activities that people like?

SPEED SOUNDS

ull

all

PRACTICE WORDS

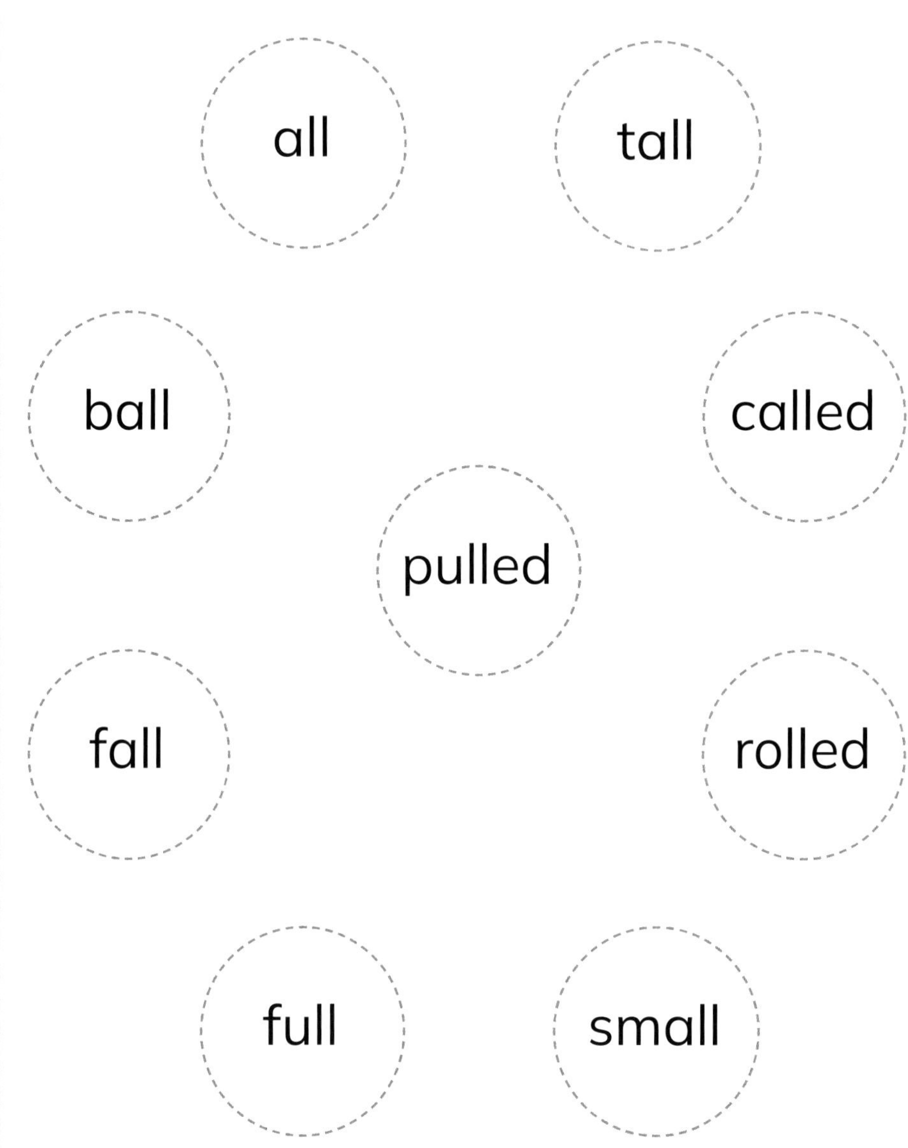